This book belongs to:

...... Eleanor ....

Lucy lives at 64 Zoo Lane, right next door to the zoo. Every night, she climbs out of her window, slides down the long long neck of Georgina the Giraffe and listens to one of the animals tell her a story. . .

...and tonight it's the

To mama – A.V.

HENRIETTA THE HAIRY HIPPO
written and illustrated by An Vrombaut
Book based on 'The Story of Henrietta the Hairy Hippo' of the TV series
64 Zoo Lane written by An Vrombaut and John Grace.
The 64 Zoo Lane song: lyrics by An Vrombaut, music by Rowland Lee, published by Millimages S.A.

First published in 2003
This paperback edition published in 2013

Copyright © Millimages S.A./ Zoo Lane Productions Ltd 2003

Hodder Children's Books
338 Euston Road
London NW1 3BH
Hodder Children's Books Australia
Level 17/207 Kent Street
Sydney, NSW 2000

A catalogue record of this book is available from the British Library.

ISBN: 978 1 444 91299 9
10 9 8 7 6 5 4 3 2 1

Printed in China

Hodder Children's Books is a division of Hachette Children's Books.
An Hachette UK Company
www.hachette.co.uk

story of

Henrietta
the
Hairy
Hippo

An Vrombaut

Hodder
Children's
Books

A division of Hachette Children's Books

The hippos in the Zambam River loved to swim in the shallow water. They rolled and splashed, plunged and splattered. But Henrietta didn't play with the others. . .

'Henrietta's hairy! Henrietta's hairy!'

sang the hippo choir all day long.
Henrietta was sad. 'I want to live somewhere
else,' she said, 'where no one laughs at me.'

And so she left the Zambam River
to find a new home.

She walked and walked
until she reached the desert.

It was hot there.

VERY HOT!

Henrietta wanted to swim, but there was no water in the desert – only a lot of sand.

'Hello there!' said a friendly voice. 'I'm Dennis the Camel. What sort of animal are you?'

'I'm Henrietta Hippo,' said Henrietta.
'And I'm looking for somewhere to live,
but the desert is TOO HOT...'

'Follow me!' said Dennis. 'You can walk in
my shadow. It's cooler there.'

And so Henrietta walked with Dennis until
she reached the jungle.

Henrietta liked the jungle. It was full of sweet smells and pretty colours. Then suddenly she heard a noise.

'CATCH US IF YOU CA-AN!'

called two monkeys.

They wanted to play!

Henrietta chased the monkeys.
She ran faster
and faster
and faster...

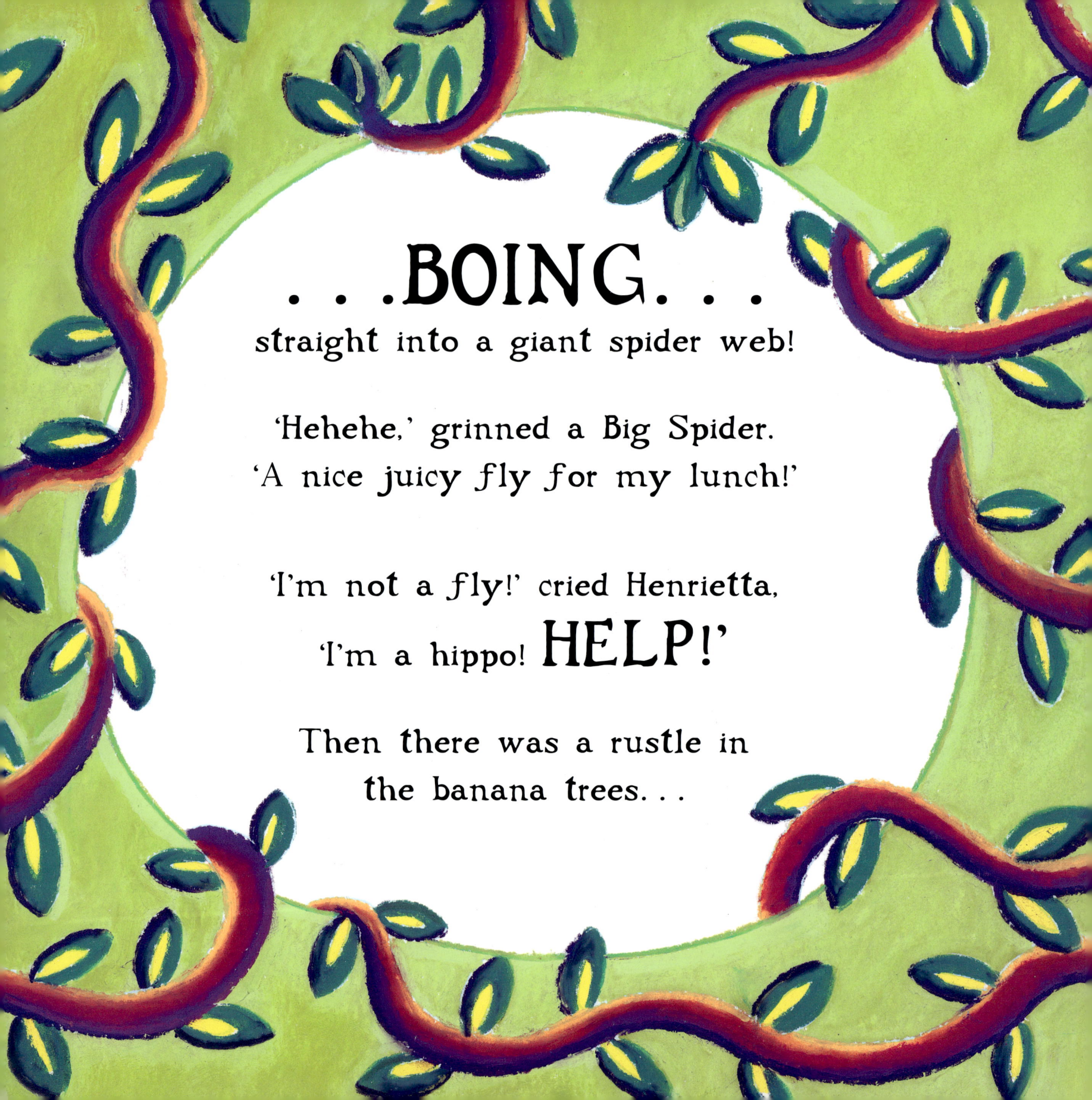

. . .BOING. . .

straight into a giant spider web!

'Hehehe,' grinned a Big Spider.
'A nice juicy fly for my lunch!'

'I'm not a fly!' cried Henrietta,
'I'm a hippo! HELP!'

Then there was a rustle in
the banana trees. . .

'BOO!' said an Even Bigger Spider and scared the Big Spider away.

'Don't worry,' said the Even Bigger Spider to Henrietta. 'It's only your monkey friends, Giggles and Tickles!' And they used their clever fingers to pull the spider web away.

'I'm Henrietta Hippo,' said Henrietta. 'And I'm looking for somewhere to live, but the jungle is TOO SCARY. . .'

'Follow us!' said the monkeys.

And so Henrietta walked with Giggles and Tickles until she reached the Blue Mountain.

The Blue Mountain
was steep and slippery.

Henrietta struggled
and scrambled
and climbed
and clambered.

Finally she reached the top.

OH, what a view!
She could see the jungle
and the desert and far, far
away, the hippos, splashing
in the Zambam River.

'If only I could go home,' she sighed.
'But I can't, because the other
hippos will laugh at
my horrible hair.'

'Well, I think you have beautiful hair!' squeaked a voice. 'You just need a new hairdo. Leave it to your friend the Snipsnip Bird!'

'Comb and snip and comb and snip,

I'll give you a look that's really hip.

. . .DONE!'

Henrietta was very pleased with
her princess hairdo.
'Thank you Snipsnip Bird!'
she said. 'Now I can go home!'

She waved goodbye and walked back
to the Zambam River.

'Henrietta!' called the other hippos. 'You look like a princess! Come over and tell us where you've been!'

And so Henrietta talked and talked as she swam across the Zambam River. She talked about the **desert.** And about the **jungle** and the **Blue Mountain**… And still the other hippos wanted to hear more!

Henrietta was very happy. But when she stepped out of the water and shook her wet coat…

. . .her princess hairdo was ruined!

Henrietta was worried. Would the other hippos laugh at her again?

But they didn't; they smiled at her!

'Come on Henrietta!' they said. 'Tell us more about your adventures.'

And so she did. And when she finished, all the hippos jumped in the Zambam River with a great big. . .

SPLASH!

Enter the wonderful world of
64 Zoo Lane with these six classic stories:

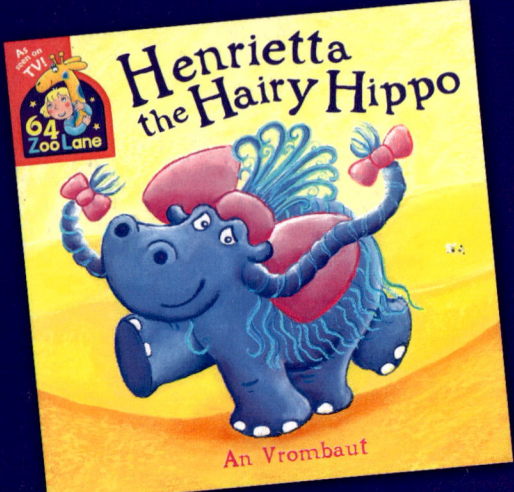

978 1 444 91299 9

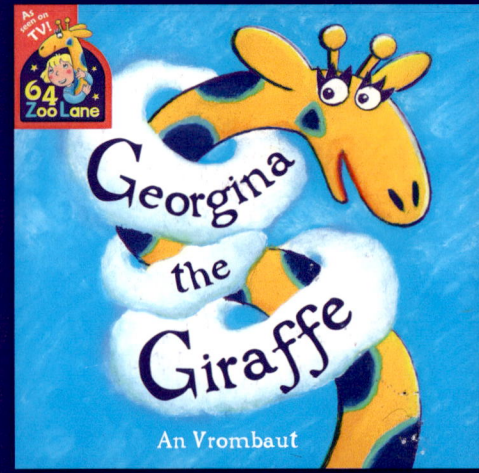

978 1 444 91298 2

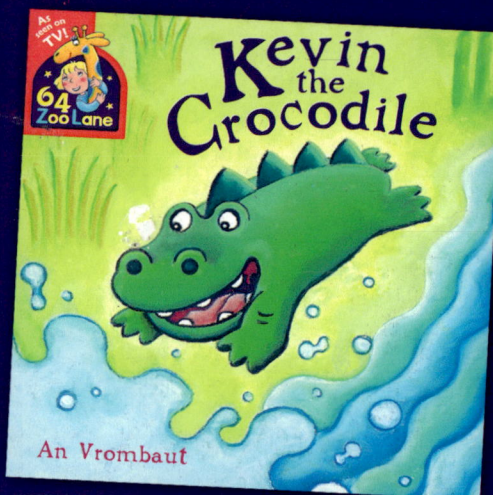

978 1 444 91301 9

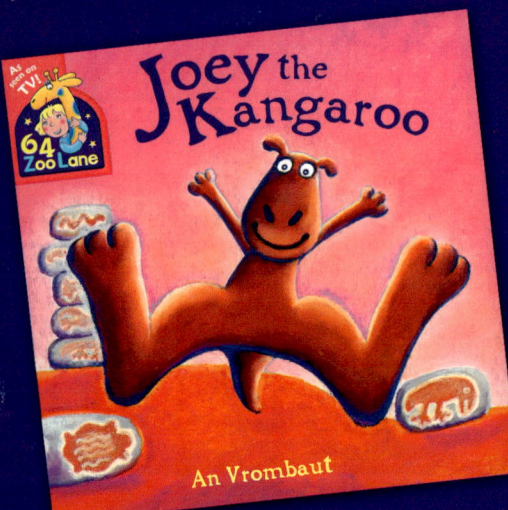

978 1 444 91300 2

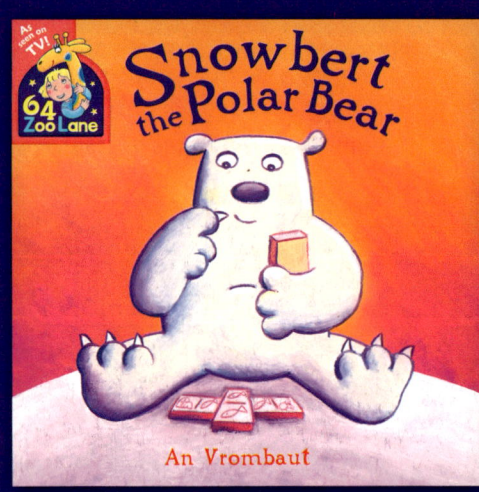

978 1 444 91302 6

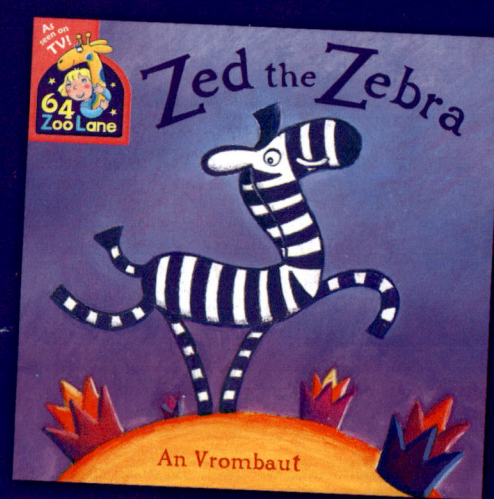

978 1 444 91303 3

Have fun with your 64 Zoo Lane friends at
www.bbc.co.uk/cbeebies/64-zoo-lane